Mapping Our World

Europe and the
Middle East

by
Fran Sammis

Benchmark Books

MARSHALL CAVENDISH
NEW YORK

Marshall Cavendish Corporation
99 White Plains Road
Tarrytown, New York 10591-9001

© Marshall Cavendish Corporation 1999

Series created by Blackbirch Graphics, Inc.

Photo Credits

Page 13: International Stock/© Roberto Arakaki; page 19 (left): George F. Mobley; pages 19 (right), 34: James L. Stanfield; page 24: Peter Arnold, Inc./© Walter H. Hodge; page 40: Peter Arnold, Inc./© Horst Schafer; page 45: International Stock/© Michael Philip Manheim; page 54: International Stock/© Bob Jacobson; page 56: International Stock/© Andre Jenny; page 58: International Stock/© J. G. Edmanson

Printed in Hong Kong

Library of Congress Cataloging-in-Publication Data

Sammis, Fran.
    Europe and the Middle East / by Fran Sammis
        p.   cm. — (Mapping our world)
    Includes bibliographical references and index.
    Summary: Presents information about the physical features, climate, land use, political divisions, religions, languages, population, transportation, plants, animals, and other aspects of Europe and the Middle East.
    ISBN 0-7614-0370-1
    1. Cartography—Europe—Juvenile literature. 2. Cartography—Middle East—Juvenile literature. [1. Cartography—Europe. 2. Cartography—Middle East. 3. Europe—Maps. 4. Middle East—Maps.] I. Title. II. Series: Sammis, Fran. Mapping our world.
    GA781.S26   1998
    940—dc21   98-11183
                                                      CIP
                                                       AC

Contents

Introduction: The Importance of Maps . .5

Chapter 1   Mapping Natural Zones and Regions . . .11

Chapter 2   Mapping People, Cultures,
and the Political World 33

Chapter 3   Mapping the World Through
Which We Move 51

Glossary 62

Further Reading 63

Index 63

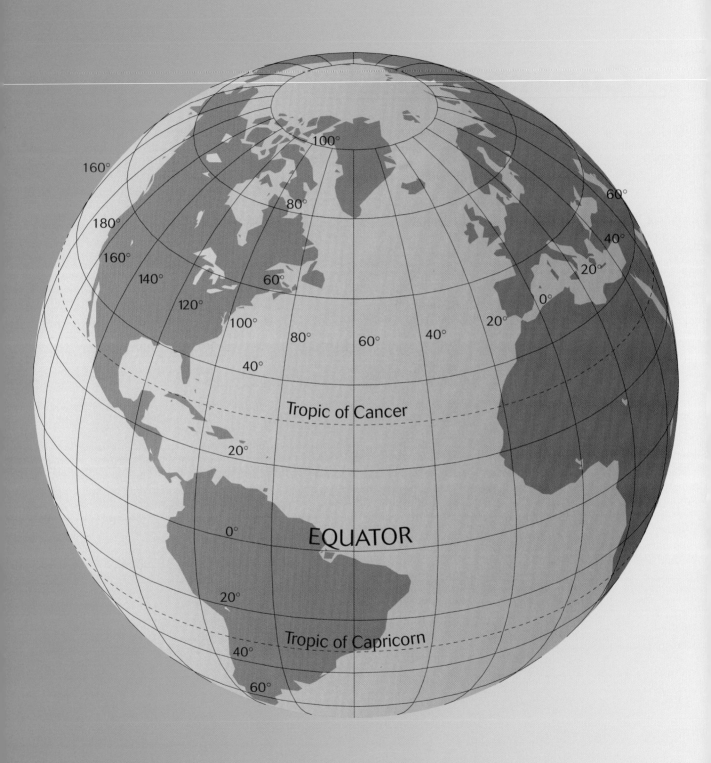

160°

180°

160°

140°

120°

100°

40°

20°

100°

80°

60°

Tropic of Cancer

0°

EQUATOR

20°

Tropic of Capricorn

40°

60°

80°

60°

40°

20°

0°

20°

40°

60°

The Importance of Maps

As tools for understanding and navigating the world around us, maps are an essential resource. Maps provide us with a representation of a place, drawn or printed on a flat surface. The place that is shown may be as vast as the solar system or as small as a neighborhood park. What we learn about the place depends on the kind of map we are using.

Kinds of Maps

Physical maps show what the land itself looks like. These maps can be used to locate and identify natural geographic features such as mountains, bodies of water, deserts, and forests.

Distribution maps show where something can be found. There are two kinds of distribution maps. One shows the range or area a feature covers, such as a map showing where grizzly bears live or where hardwood forests grow.

The second kind of distribution map shows the density of a feature. That is, how much or how little of the feature is present. These maps allow us to see patterns in the way a feature is distributed. Rainfall and population maps are two examples of this kind of distribution map.

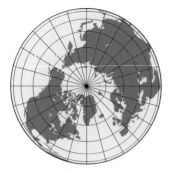

Globular

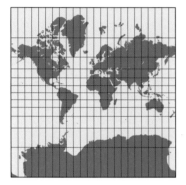

Mercator

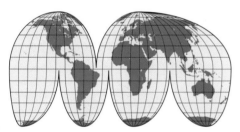

Mollweide

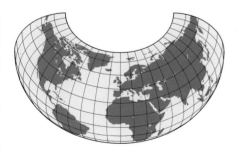

Armadillo

Political maps show us how an area is divided into countries, states, provinces, or other units. They also show where cities and towns are located. Major highways and transportation routes are also included on some kinds of political maps.

Movement maps help us find our way around. They can be road maps, street maps, and public transportation maps. Special movement maps called "charts" are used by airplane or boat pilots to navigate through air or on water.

Why Maps Are Important

Many people depend on maps to do their jobs. A geologist, for example, uses maps of Earth's structure to locate natural resources such as coal or petroleum. A transportation planner will use population maps to determine where new roads may need to be built.

A map can tell us how big a place is, where one place is in relation to another, what a place was like in the past, and what it's like now. Maps help us understand and move through our own part of the world and the rest of the world, too. Some maps even help us move through our solar system and universe!

Terms to Know

Maps are created and designed by incorporating many different elements and accepted cartographic (mapmaking) techniques. Often, maps showing the exact same area will differ from one another, depending upon the choice or critical elements, such as scale and projection. Following is a brief listing of some key mapmaking terms.

Projection. A projection is a way to represent the round Earth on a flat surface. There are a number of different ways to project, or transfer, round-Earth information to a flat surface, though each method results in some distortion. That is, areas may appear larger or smaller than they really are—or closer or farther apart. The maps on page 6 show a few varieties of projections.

Latitude. Lines of latitude, or parallels, run parallel to the equator (the imaginary center of Earth's circumference) and are used to locate points north and south of the equator. The equator is 0 degrees latitude, the north pole is 90 degrees north latitude, and the south pole is 90 degrees south latitude.

Longitude. Lines of longitude, or meridians, run at right angles to the equator and meet at the north and south poles. Lines of longitude are used to locate points east and west of the prime meridian.

Prime meridian. An imaginary line that runs through Greenwich, England; considered 0 degrees longitude. Lines to the west of the prime meridian go halfway around the world to 180 degrees west longitude; lines to the east go to 180 degrees east longitude.

Hemisphere. A half circle. Dividing the world in half from pole to pole along the prime meridian gives you the eastern and western hemispheres. Dividing the world in half at the equator gives you the northern and southern hemispheres.

Scale. The relationship of distance on a map to the actual distance on the ground. Scale can be expressed in three ways:

1. As a ratio—1:63,360 (one inch equals 63,360 inches)
2. Verbally—one inch equals one mile
3. Graphically— ⌐ 1 mi. ⌐

Because 63,360 inches equal one mile, these scales give the same information: one map-inch equals one mile on the ground.

Large-scale maps show a small area, such as a city park, in great detail. Small-scale maps show a large area, such as an entire continent, in much less detail, and on a much smaller scale.

The Art and Process of Mapmaking

Maps have been made for thousands of years. Early maps, based on first-hand exploration, were some of the most accurate tools of their

◀◀ Opposite: The maps shown here are just four of the many different projections in which the world can be displayed.

225 million years ago

1

180 million years ago

2

65 million years ago

3

present day

4

time. Others, based on guesses about what an area was like, were often very beautiful, but were not especially accurate.

As technology—such as photography and flight—evolved, cartographers (mapmakers) were able not only to map most of Earth in detail, they were also able to make maps of our solar system.

To make a map today, cartographers first determine what a map is to show and who is most likely to use it. Then, they assemble the information they will need for the map, which can come from many different kinds of experts—such as meteorologists, geologists, and surveyors—as well as from aerial photography or satellite feedback.

Mapping a Changing Earth

If you traced around all the land masses shown on a world map, then cut them out and put them together like a jigsaw puzzle, the result would look something like map 1 at the top of this page. Scientists think this is how Earth looked about 225 million years ago.

Over time, this single continent, Pangaea (Pan–JEE–uh), slowly broke apart into two land masses called Laurasia and Gondwanaland (map 2). Maps 3 and 4 show how the land masses continued to break up and drift apart over millions of years, until the continents assumed the shapes and positions we recognize today. Earth has not, however, finished changing.

Scientists have established that Earth's surface is made up of sections called tectonic plates. These rigid plates, shown in the map on page 9, are in

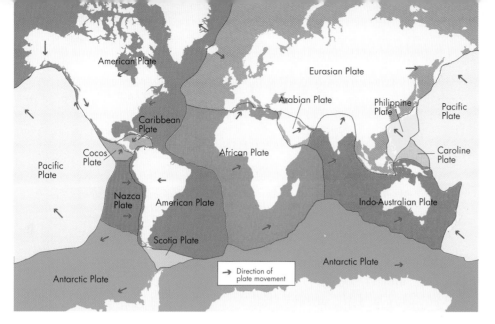

◀ **Left:** *The tectonic plates that lie beneath Earth's surface are in a slow but constant motion.*

◀◀ **Opposite:** *The continents of our planet were once clumped together but have spread apart over millions of years in what is called continental drift.*

slow constant motion, moving from 1/4 to 1 inch a year. As they move, they take the continents and sea floors with them. Sometimes, their movements cause disasters, such as earthquakes and volcanic activity.

After many more millions of years have passed, our Earth's continents will again look very different from what we know today.

Reading a Map

In order for a map to be useful, it must be the right kind of map for the job. A small-scale map of Illinois would not help you find your way around Chicago; for that, you would need a large-scale map of the city. A physical map of North America would not tell you where most of the people live; you would need a distribution map that shows population.

Once you have found the right map, you will need to refer to the map legend, or key, to be sure you are interpreting the map's information correctly. Depending on the type of map, the legend tells the scale used for the map, and notes the meaning of any symbols and colors used.

In their most basic form, maps function as place finders. They show us where places are, and we use these maps to keep from getting lost. But as you have begun to see, maps can tell us much more about our world than simply where places are located. Just how much more, you'll discover in the chapters ahead.

Physical Map
of Europe

Key

Feet (meters)
above sea level

20 (6)
1,000 (305)
5,000 (1,524)
10,000 (3,048)

Arctic Ocean

URAL MOUNTAINS

ICELAND

SWEDEN

NORWAY

FINLAND

Baltic Sea

ESTONIA

Volga

RUSSIA (partial)

Atlantic Ocean

North Sea

DENMARK

LATVIA

LITHUANIA

RUSSIA

Don

IRELAND

NETHERLANDS

BELARUS

KAZAKHSTAN (partial)

UNITED KINGDOM

GERMANY

POLAND

Oder

Dnepr

LUXEMBOURG

BELGIUM

Rhine

UKRAINE

Seine

CZECH REPUBLIC

CARPATHIAN MTS.

FRANCE

SLOVAKIA

AUSTRIA

HUNGARY

SWITZERLAND

Po

MOLDOVA

PORTUGAL

CANTABRIAN MTS.

PYRENEES

Rhone

ROMANIA

Black Sea

CROATIA

SLOVENIA

YUGOSLAVIA

Danube

ITALY

BOSNIA & HERZEGOVINA

BULGARIA

SPAIN

ALBANIA

MACEDONIA

TURKEY

GREECE

TAURUS

SYRIA

Mediterranean Sea

The
Middle
East

Black Sea

BULGARIA

GEORGIA

CAUCASUS MTS.

ARMENIA

AZERBAIJAN

TURKEY

Caspian Sea

CYPRUS

Euphrates

Tigris

LEBANON

SYRIA

IRAQ

IRAN

Mediterranean Sea

ISRAEL

Dead Sea

JORDAN

KUWAIT

Persian Gulf

BAHRAIN

QATAR

UNITED ARAB EMIRATES

SAUDI ARABIA

Red Sea

OMAN

YEMEN

Gulf of Aden

Indian Ocean

Europe and the
Middle East

URAL MTS.

Ural River

Chapter 1

Mapping Natural Zones and Regions

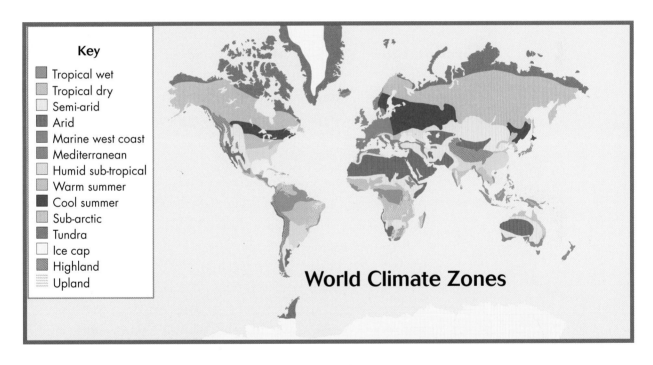

Key

- Tropical wet
- Tropical dry
- Semi-arid
- Arid
- Marine west coast
- Mediterranean
- Humid sub-tropical
- Warm summer
- Cool summer
- Sub-arctic
- Tundra
- Ice cap
- Highland
- Upland

World Climate Zones

Europe covers approximately 4,200,000 square miles (6,759,060 square kilometers). This is about the size of the United States—with an extra Alaska added to it. Europe's western boundary is the Atlantic Ocean; the eastern boundary is made up of the Ural Mountains, the Ural River, and the Caspian Sea. This boundary includes only part of Russia. As a result, there is a European Russia and an Asian Russia.

▲ *Above: The dry climate of the Middle East is similar to that of North Africa and of the southwestern United States.*

◄◄ *Opposite: The Ural Mountains, the Ural River, and the Caspian Sea mark the boundary between Europe and Asia.*

On the north, Europe is bounded by the Arctic Ocean, and on the south, by the Mediterranean Sea, the Black Sea, and the Caucasus Mountains, which stretch across northern Georgia and Azerbaijan. Iceland, the British Isles, and many other islands off the mainland are also considered part of Europe.

Although Europe has traditionally been called a continent, it doesn't fit the geographical definition of a continent: a large body of land surrounded by water. Since Europe is really an extension of Asia, some people consider the two regions to be one continent—Eurasia. Most, however, continue to think of Europe as a separate body of land because of its historical importance.

The Boundaries of the Middle East

The Middle East is the term commonly given to the southwestern extension of Asia. This area stretches from Georgia and Azerbaijan, south to the Arabian Sea and the Gulf of Aden. The western boundary is the Red Sea and the Mediterranean Sea; the northern boundary is the Black Sea.

Although the extreme northwest corner of Turkey and the northernmost edges of Georgia and Azerbaijan actually lie within the boundaries of Europe, these countries are considered Middle Eastern.

Some African countries—especially Egypt—are thought of as part of the Middle East. There is no agreement on which countries to include, however. Africa is covered in another volume in this series, and the countries within its physical boundaries are discussed there.

To learn about what Europe and the Middle East are like, you might start by referring to maps that show their physical features (topography), climate, land use, and other natural characteristics.

The Topography of Europe

Of the four major physical regions that cover Europe, three feature mountains (colored brown on the physical map). The Northwest Uplands, as the name implies, cuts across the northwestern part of

Europe. This is a rugged, mountainous region with high plateaus and deep valleys. It runs from the far western point of France through Ireland and northern Great Britain, on into Denmark, Sweden, and the northern part of Finland.

Low mountains and plateaus are found in the Central Uplands. This region covers the central and southern portions of Spain and Portugal, central France and Germany, almost all of the Czech Republic, and a sliver of southwestern Poland.

The third mountainous region consists of the Alpine Mountain system, which thrusts its way eastward across southern Europe from Spain to the Black Sea. This region also takes in the northern edge of the Caucasus Mountains, spanning the area between the Black and Caspian Seas.

In addition to the Caucasus, the Alpine system includes several other mountain chains. The most famous is the Alps, which cover part of southeastern France, northern Italy, most of Switzerland and Austria, southern Germany, and northern Slovenia. The Alps are very popular with vacationers from all over the world. In summer, the beautiful snow-capped mountains and flower-filled meadows draw many hikers and walkers; in winter, skiers flock to scenic Alpine resorts.

As you can tell from the physical map on page 10, the remaining portion of Europe has a much different look to it. This Central Plain consists of flat or gently rolling land—quite a contrast to the Upland

▼ *Below: The Dolomite Alps, in Italy, provide a dramatic backdrop for Misurina Lake.*

and Alpine regions! The Central Plain starts out as a narrow band running along western France, continues up through Belgium, The Netherlands, Germany, and Poland. From Poland the plain spreads out broadly, extending east to the Ural Mountains, north to the Arctic Ocean, and south to the Black Sea and the Caucasus Mountains. The Central Plain region also covers the southeast section of England.

In addition to its abundance of mountains, Europe has a great many rivers. Several of the world's principal rivers are located there, among them, the Volga and the Danube. The Volga, Europe's longest river at 2,291 miles (3,687 kilometers), flows through Russia to the Caspian Sea. The Danube is Europe's second-longest river. It flows 1,766 miles (2,842 kilometers) in a winding path from southern Germany, through Austria, Slovakia, Hungary, Yugoslavia, Bulgaria, and Romania, ending at the Black Sea.

Among the many other important rivers of Europe are the Rhine, which flows from the German Alps through The Netherlands to the North Sea; the Dnepr, which runs through Russia, Belarus, and Ukraine; and the Don, in Russia. The most important rivers in France are the Rhone and Seine; in Poland, the Oder; and in Italy, the Po.

The Caspian Sea, which lies partly in Europe and partly in Asia, is actually misnamed. Because it is surrounded by land, the Caspian is a lake, not a sea. In fact, it is the world's largest lake and the lowest point in Europe. The Caspian Sea received its Italian name—*Mare Caspium*—from the Romans. They called it a sea (*mare*) because it contains saltwater, not freshwater.

The Topography of the Middle East

Like Europe, the Middle East has four main physical regions. Aside from the mountains to the north, however, the topography of the Middle East is very different from that of Europe.

Mountains and rugged, dry plateaus cover most of the northern Middle East, including Turkey, Armenia, Azerbaijan, Georgia, and Iran. This topographical region is colored brown on the map on page 10.

A major fertile coastal strip, colored dark green, is located along the eastern Mediterranean in Lebanon, Israel, and Syria.

The third main physical region is the delta of southeastern Iraq. This is formed by the joined Tigris and Euphrates Rivers as the system empties into the Persian Gulf. These two rivers are the principal rivers in the Middle East.

Desert areas cover much of the rest of the Middle East, and some of the world's hottest and driest deserts are located there. The Arabian Peninsula—which includes Saudi Arabia, Yemen, Oman, the United Arab Emirates, Qatar, and Kuwait—is almost entirely desert. In southern Saudi Arabia, you'll find the world's largest continuous sand desert—the Rub al-Khali. It covers over 200,000 square miles (518,000 square kilometers). In some parts of the desert, sand dunes rise more than 500 feet (152 meters) high—the height of a 50-story building.

The Middle East is also home to the world's lowest point of elevation, the Dead Sea. This body of water, located between Israel and Jordan, is 1,290 feet below sea level.

Climate and Weather

The physical traits of Europe and the Middle East are affected by the region's climate. Climate and weather are not the same thing. Weather is short-lived; it changes from day to day. Climate is the average characteristics of the weather in a given place over a long period of time. Although climates can change, they do so much more slowly than weather—over many years, rather than days.

Meteorologists use a variety of high-tech methods to gather the information that allows them to analyze and predict the weather. Among those methods are sophisticated ways of viewing and mapping the world.

Analyzing and Predicting Weather

The major elements that are used to describe the weather and categorize climate are: temperature, precipitation, humidity, amount of sunshine, wind, and air pressure.

Manned and unmanned weather stations on land and at sea, weather balloons, airplanes, and satellites are all used in gathering weather information for analysis. Radar, cameras, and thermal infrared sensors monitor and record the weather conditions.

The information from these sources is sent to weather centers throughout the world by means of a worldwide satellite system, called the Global Telecommunications System (GTS). The information is fed into computers that record and analyze the data, which can then be compiled into highly detailed and informative maps. The GTS also allows weather centers to share their data.

By studying global weather patterns over a long time, climatologists can map climatic regions—areas that have similar climates. The world climate zones map on page 11 is just one example of this kind of map.

The Climate of Europe and the Middle East

The climate of Europe and the Middle East ranges from constantly cold to blazingly hot—from average summer highs of 35 degrees Fahrenheit (2 degrees Celsius) in arctic regions to 125 degrees Fahrenheit (52 degrees Celsius) in the deserts of the Arabian Peninsula.

- The tundra regions of northern Europe are always cold, and have little precipitation at any time. There is a summer season, but it is very short and chilly. This is the only time of year that the ground isn't frozen, and, even then, only the topmost layer thaws.

- The sub-arctic climate (colored light purple) features a short, cool summer and a long, cold winter. Light to moderate precipitation occurs mainly in the summer.

- Much of the interior of Europe has a moist, continental climate. This area, shown in dark blue on the climate map and referred to as "cool summer," experiences cool summers and cold winters. In this region, precipitation is moderate year-round.

- Most of the rest of Europe is influenced by winds blowing in from the Atlantic Ocean. These winds are first warmed by the Gulf Stream—an ocean current that flows from the Gulf of Mexico in a

▶▶ *Opposite: Western European countries enjoy a comfortable, mild climate.*

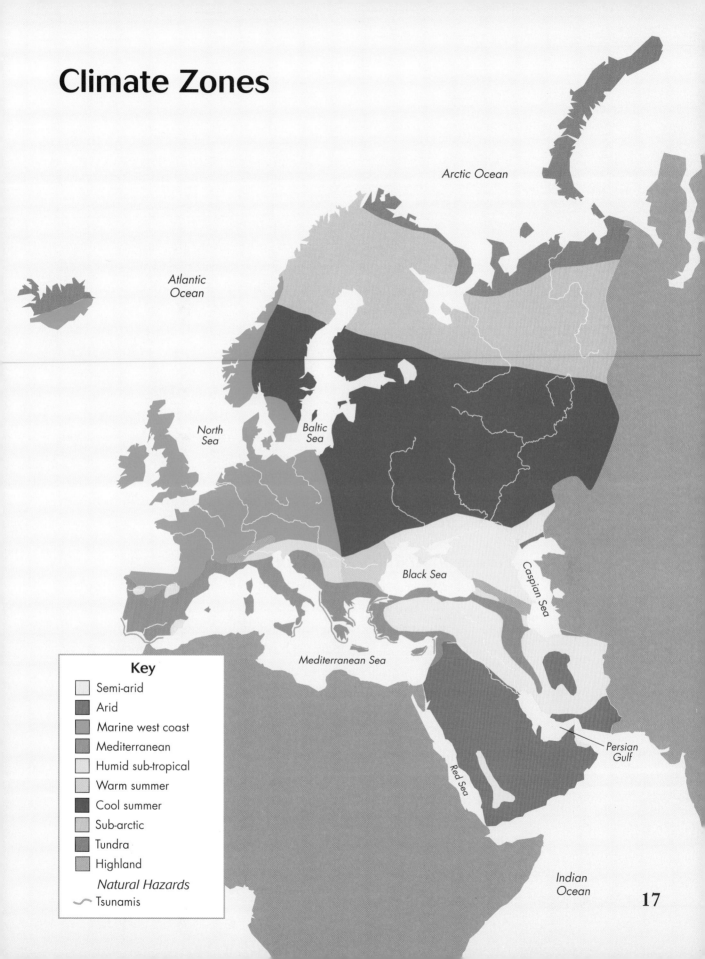

Climate Zones

Arctic Ocean

Atlantic
Ocean

North
Sea

Baltic
Sea

Black Sea

Caspian Sea

Mediterranean Sea

Red Sea

Persian
Gulf

Indian
Ocean

Key

- Semi-arid
- Arid
- Marine west coast
- Mediterranean
- Humid sub-tropical
- Warm summer
- Cool summer
- Sub-arctic
- Tundra
- Highland

Natural Hazards
- Tsunamis

17

northeasterly direction to western Europe. The result is a mild climate in most of western Europe, with moderately warm summers and cool winters. Precipitation is moderate throughout the year. This region, considered "marine west coast," is colored turquoise on the climate map.

- The warmest European climate is found along the Mediterranean Sea. There the summers are hot and dry, and the winters are mild and rainy. The "Mediterranean" climate is colored medium blue on the map.

- Parts of the Middle East, particularly around the Mediterranean and Black Seas, also have a Mediterranean climate. The rugged mountain areas in the north, however, are high enough to get snow. Overall, the Middle East is simply hot and dry. You can see this by looking at the map on page 17. Most of the Middle East is either semi-arid (gold) or arid (red). The semi-arid areas receive only about 10 to 15 inches (25 to 38 centimeters) of precipitation a year, while the arid areas receive even less. Many places in these climate zones have summer temperatures of more than 100 degrees Fahrenheit (38 degrees Celsius).

European Animals and Plants

A lot of the large wild animals that used to roam freely over Europe—such as the European bison—are now found mainly in preserves, parks, and zoos. Hunting has thinned this animal population, and the growth of cities, industry, and agriculture has destroyed their habitats.

Among the animals to be found in the cold climate of northern Europe are reindeer, brown bears, and, on islands in the Arctic Ocean, polar bears. The Norway lemming—a furry, mouselike rodent known for making long migrations in great numbers—is native only to Europe. The goatlike chamois and ibex make their homes in the mountains of southwestern Europe, and wild sheep live in the mountains of Italy.

In the more temperate regions of Europe, you'll find a greater variety of animals. Eastern Europe is home to wolves and wild boars.

Throughout western Europe, foxes, badgers, hedgehogs, hares (larger than rabbits and with longer ears and legs), moles, otters, and various kinds of deer are common.

Many edible fish, such as tuna, mackerel, cod, and sardines, are found in European waters, particularly the Atlantic Ocean and the North Sea. Sturgeon, valued especially for their eggs, are caught in the Caspian Sea.

Native European birds include the nightingale, finch, house sparrow, raven, cuckoo, and stork, a large wading bird. It is often considered a sign of good luck to have storks nest on your chimney!

Modern civilization has affected Europe's plant life as well as its animal life. Immense forests once covered most of Europe, but they were cut down over the centuries for fuel and lumber and to clear land for cities and farms. Most of the remaining large forests of pine and spruce trees are in northern Europe. They stretch from Norway eastward across Russia. In the far northern tundra areas, the frozen landscape only comes to life during the brief summer season, when you can find wildflowers and lichens and mosses brightening the landscape.

The open Central Plain region is grassland. Short grasses grow in the dry areas of southwestern Russia. Longer grasses are found in the rest of the region.

Some deciduous, or mixed evergreen and deciduous, forests are found in western and southern Europe, especially around the mountains. This area also contains a well-known evergreen forest—the Black Forest of southwestern Germany. The trees of the Mediterranean region include cypress and olive trees, which thrive in a warm, sunny climate.

▲ ◀ *Above left: A reindeer in a field in Norway is poised to run.*

▲ ▶ *Above right: This lovely Cedar of Lebanon was photographed in a grove near the Mediterranean coast.*

Middle Eastern Animals and Plants

In the mountains of the Middle East live wild sheep, mountain goats, and the beautiful, thick-furred snow leopard. Like the temperate areas of Europe, Middle Eastern forests are home to many different animals. For example, the forests near the coasts of the Mediterranean and Black Seas are home to bears, wolves, red deer, and porcupines. Many different kinds of warblers—small, colorful songbirds—nest in the woodlands of Syria and Lebanon.

The less harsh desert areas are home to a variety of wildlife. Here you might see cheetahs, hyraxes, gerbils, jerboas, Pallas' cats, gazelles, beetles, and snakes. In the Red Sea and Persian Gulf, coral reefs provide shelter for turtles and hundreds of colorful tropical fish.

The plants of the Middle East vary considerably from one climate zone to the next. Dwarf shrubs and grasses are the main plant life of the rugged northern mountain areas. Where the climate and landscape are more moderate, near the Mediterranean and Black Seas, for example, there are oak, pine, and cedar woodlands. The Cedars of Lebanon are world famous for their beauty. Because the Tigris-Euphrates lowlands flood periodically, this area contains trees that tolerate wet conditions, such as poplars and willows.

The interior parts of the deserts with the harshest climate are bare of plant life. In other areas, however, the ground is scattered year-round with short shrubs and, when it rains, with a variety of brightly colored flowers.

How Climate and Topography Affect People

As we have seen, climate greatly affects plant and animal life. Of course, a region's climate and topography can affect many aspects of human life as well. Among them:

Population distribution. More people tend to settle in areas that have a mild or moderate climate, adequate rainfall, and fairly level, open land. Population will be less densely distributed in regions that are mountainous or thickly forested, and in regions with climates that are very cold or dry. You can see this connection if you compare the world climate zones map on page 11 in this chapter with the world population density map on page 33 in Chapter 2.

How people live and work. The type of housing people live in, the clothes they wear, and the kind of work they do, all depend in part on the climate of their region. The physical structure of the land also can affect what work people do. For example, large-scale farming is an option in plains areas, but not in mountainous regions.

Agriculture. To a large extent, climate dictates what crops can or can't be successfully grown in an area. Using technology, such as artificial irrigation or greenhouses, can change the impact of weather and climate to a degree. However, agriculture is most successful when crops are naturally suited to the area in which they are grown.

Transportation. An area's climate and topography can dictate which forms of transportation are used there. For example, dogsleds are an obvious choice in arctic areas, while camels or elephants are well suited to travel in hot, arid conditions. More roads and railroads will be built in areas that have a level terrain, as opposed to mountainous areas.

Economy. Some areas, such as deserts, have little or no natural resources. These areas have a climate or topography that doesn't allow for extensive agriculture or a developed transportation system. Such harsh regions will most likely be poorer than areas that can support industry, large-scale agriculture, or other means of making a living and engaging in trade.

The Land and the People of Europe and the Middle East

In Europe and the Middle East, as elsewhere in the world, the majority of people have adapted to the land by choosing to settle in areas that have moderate climates and flat or rolling terrain. This connection can be seen by comparing the physical, climate, and population density maps on pages 10, 17, and 48. Some peoples, however, have made special adjustments in order to live in less agreeable areas.

The people of Kuwait, in the Middle East, have worked out ways to grow food in spite of their land, which is mostly barren desert unsuited to farming. They use hothouse systems outfitted for hydroponic gardening—growing plants in water rather than soil.

Although flat land is usually preferred for settlements, sometimes land can be too flat. This is the case in The Netherlands. Much of the land along the North Sea is not just flat; in many places it is lower than sea level and prone to flooding. By building a series of dikes to hold back the water, and pumping the land dry, the Nederlanders have been able to reclaim the rich soil for farming.

At Iran's eastern edge, people have adapted their houses to the climate in a special way: The houses are built without north-facing windows. They are built this way because severe dust storms blow in from the north in the summer. In a normal summer, there will be 80 days when dust storms fill the air. Houses stay much cleaner without windows in their north walls.

The Land and the Economy

Europe's land is valuable to its economy as a source of both agriculture and mining. In the Middle East, the land is most valuable for its mineral resources, particularly oil.

Crops

Some of the world's richest farmland is found in Europe. Crops are grown on much of the continent, as the land use map on the opposite page shows. The most fertile area is the Central Plain. Here wheat is the most important grain crop. Barley, potatoes, rye, and sugar beets are also valuable.

In the Mediterranean area of Europe, olives, citrus fruits, and grapes are important. In France and Italy, grapes are grown to make wine that is exported all over the world.

A very different kind of crop is important to The Netherlands: flowers! Huge fields of colorful blooms are grown to be sold as cut

▶▶ *Opposite: The Middle East has fewer agricultural products than Europe, where the land is more fertile.*

Land Use

Arctic Ocean

TIMBER

TIMBER

Atlantic
Ocean

SHEEP

OATS
RYE TIMBER

TIMBER

DAIRY

DAIRY

RYE

Baltic
Sea

DAIRY

DAIRY

WHEAT

OATS
SHEEP

North
Sea

HOGS

DAIRY

OATS

POTATOES
SHEEP

DAIRY

HOGS

RYE

POTATOES

RYE

CATTLE
WHEAT

WHEAT FLOWERS

POTATOES

BARLEY HOGS

SUGAR BEETS

WHEAT

WHEAT

CORN

FRUIT

HOGS

GRAPES

DAIRY

GRAPES

CATTLE

CORN

Black Sea

CORN

GRAPES
OLIVES

SHEEP

Caspian Sea

GRAPES

FRUIT

GRAPES

OLIVES

WHEAT

FRUIT

OLIVES

CITRUS

GRAPES

Mediterranean Sea

CITRUS
SHEEP

WHEAT
COTTON
SHEEP

WHEAT

Persian
Gulf

Red Sea

DATES

DATES

COFFEE

Indian
Ocean

Key

- Cropland
- Irrigated land
- Grazing land
- Forest, woodland
- Desert vegetation
- Wetland, swamp
- Barren land

23

▶ *Right:* The Netherlands is famous for its tulips. Dutch tulip bulbs are sold around the world.

▶▶ *Opposite:* Northern and western Europe are rich in iron and lignite.

flowers or bulbs. The tulips that are so closely associated with Holland were actually first cultivated in the Middle East, in Turkey.

As you can see from the land use map, crops are grown on a small fraction of land in the Middle East, mostly near the coasts of the Mediterranean, Black, and Caspian Seas. In northern Iraq, cereal grains are important. In Syria, lentils, barley, and sugar beets are grown. Cotton is Syria's main cash crop. Turkey is among the world's largest suppliers of figs, hazelnuts, and oriental tobacco. Citrus fruits are a major cash crop for both Israel and Lebanon.

Dairy products are important to the European economy, particularly cheeses, which are exported worldwide. Fishing is not a land-based activity, but should be mentioned here because of its economic importance in Europe. The major European fishing grounds are in the Atlantic Ocean, the North Sea, and the Arctic Ocean. Norway and Russia are among the world's leaders of the fishing industry. Herring, cod, and sardines are important catches.

Mineral Resources

As you can see from the map on the opposite page, Europe's mineral resources are concentrated mainly in western Europe, with additional major deposits in Russia. Among the most important European mineral resources are coal and petroleum, which are discussed on page 26 under the heading Energy Production and Consumption. Iron ore, found throughout northern and western Europe, is another important mineral.

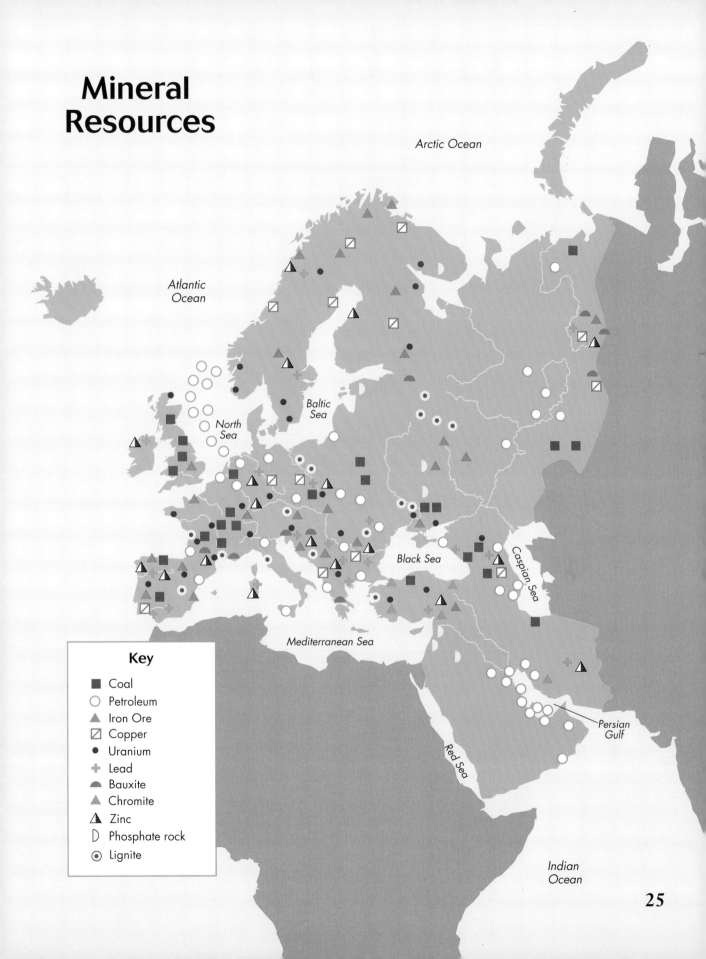

Mineral Resources

Arctic Ocean

Atlantic Ocean

Baltic Sea

North Sea

Black Sea

Caspian Sea

Mediterranean Sea

Red Sea

Persian Gulf

Indian Ocean

Key

- ■ Coal
- ○ Petroleum
- ▲ Iron Ore
- ▨ Copper
- ● Uranium
- ✚ Lead
- ◗ Bauxite
- ▲ Chromite
- ◮ Zinc
- ◗ Phosphate rock
- ◉ Lignite

25

Although the Middle East produces several different minerals, it is easy to see from the map that the most abundant is petroleum. Jordan is not rich in petroleum, but it is a major supplier of phosphates, which are used in the manufacture of fertilizers.

Energy Production and Consumption

Looking at the map on the opposite page, you can see that in Europe, gas and coal are the primary sources of energy. In addition, major oil fields and basins are located in Russia and offshore in the North Sea. Other, much less important, oil fields are scattered throughout central Europe. Nuclear power is used as a source of energy primarily in west-central Europe. While not a major energy source at the present time, the importance of nuclear power is increasing.

In the Middle East, energy is produced almost entirely from oil, as you can see from the map. This is not surprising when you consider that the Middle East contains 60 percent of the world's supply of petroleum. While oil is found throughout the region, the primary producers are Saudi Arabia, Kuwait, Oman, Qatar, and the United Arab Emirates. Natural gas fields associated with some of the oil deposits also contribute to energy production in the Middle East.

The areas that consume the most energy (see the map on page 28) are northern and eastern Europe, Germany, the United Kingdom, and most of the Arabian Peninsula. Heating, mining, industry, and oil and gas production account in large part for the heavy energy consumption in these regions. To see how Europe and the Middle East compare to the rest of the world in energy production and consumption, see the maps on page 29.

The Environment

A look at the environmental damage map on page 30 shows that one of the biggest problems in Europe is acid rain. It is a direct result of Europe's role as a major manufacturing center for the world. The gases in the atmosphere that produce acid rain come mainly from burning

▶▶ *Opposite: Nearly all of the energy produced in the Middle East is from oil and natural gas.*

Energy Production

Arctic Ocean

Atlantic Ocean

North Sea

Baltic Sea

Black Sea

Caspian Sea

Mediterranean Sea

Red Sea

Persian Gulf

Indian Ocean

Key

- • Oil fields
- ⬭ Oil basins
- ○ Minor coal fields
- ⬭ Major coal fields
- ▪ Gas fields
- ▲ Nuclear power

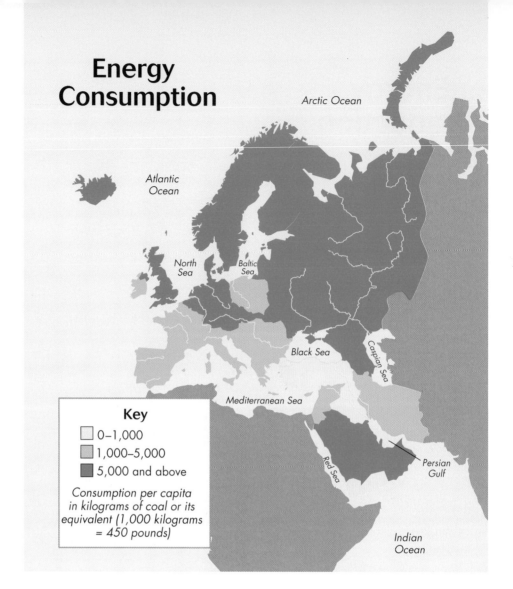

Energy Consumption

Arctic Ocean

Atlantic Ocean

North Sea

Baltic Sea

Black Sea

Caspian Sea

Mediterranean Sea

Red Sea

Persian Gulf

Indian Ocean

Key

☐ 0–1,000

▨ 1,000–5,000

▉ 5,000 and above

Consumption per capita in kilograms of coal or its equivalent (1,000 kilograms = 450 pounds)

▶ *Right: Energy is consumed heavily in the industrialized nations of Europe and in the oil-producing countries of the Arabian Peninsula.*

coal, oil, and gas to fuel homes or to power Europe's many factories. When these gases, which contain acid, meet damp air, they fall to the ground as acid rain. The problem affects both the natural and human-made environment. It weakens and destroys trees and other plants, and pollutes rivers and lakes, killing any fish that live in them. It also corrodes buildings and statues.

Another environmental problem caused in large part by industry is coastal pollution. Factory waste is responsible for much of this pollution. However, compare the energy production map on page 27 with the environmental damage map. It is easy to see that oil production also contributes to the problem of coastal pollution, particularly in the North Sea and Persian Gulf.

In the Middle East, human-induced desertification—fertile land turning to desert—is a major problem. In the area of the Tigris and Euphrates Rivers, desertification is a result of increased agricultural production. Intensive farming methods, including the increased use of chemicals, have depleted the soil.

The points of human-induced salinization marked on the map show areas where over-irrigation is damaging the land. In these

▼ *Below:* *Africa and South America are light producers and consumers of the world's energy supplies.*

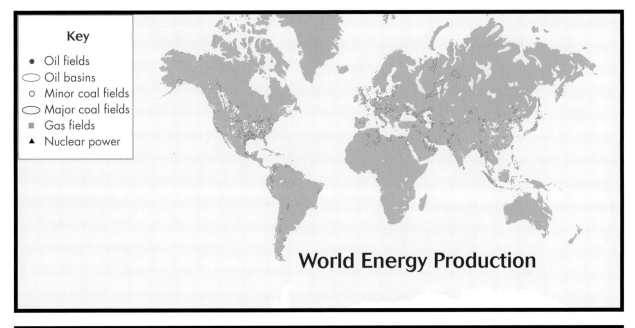

Key

- • Oil fields
- ◯ Oil basins
- ◦ Minor coal fields
- ◯ Major coal fields
- ▪ Gas fields
- ▲ Nuclear power

World Energy Production

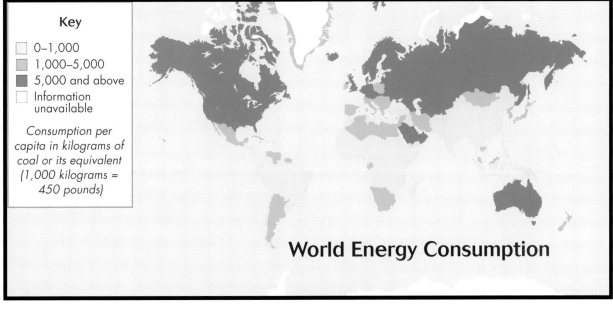

Key

- ☐ 0–1,000
- ▨ 1,000–5,000
- ■ 5,000 and above
- ☐ Information unavailable

Consumption per capita in kilograms of coal or its equivalent (1,000 kilograms = 450 pounds)

World Energy Consumption

Environmental Damage

Arctic Ocean

Atlantic Ocean

North Sea

Baltic Sea

Helsinki

Stockholm

St. Petersburg

Moscow

Glasgow

Copenhagen

Belfast

Barnsley

Amsterdam

Berlin

Warsaw

Dunkirk

Brussels

Wroclaw

Le Harve

Frankfurt

Chauny

Linz

Zaporozh'ye

Strasbourg

Bolzano

Gourdon

Lyon

Milan

Zagreb

Marseilles

Turin

Black Sea

Caspian Sea

Madrid

Lisbon

Athens

Tehran

Euphrates

Tigris

Baghdad

Persian Gulf

Mediterranean Sea

Red Sea

Indian Ocean

Key

▨	Human-induced desertification
▨	Coastal pollution
●	Human-induced salinization
▨	Area affected by acid rain
●	Selected city with high level of air pollution

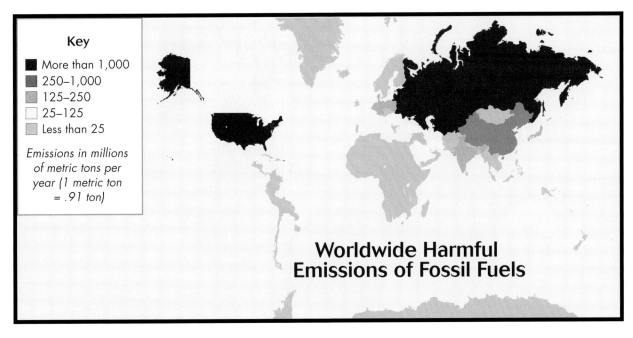

Key

- ■ More than 1,000
- ■ 250–1,000
- ■ 125–250
- ☐ 25–125
- ■ Less than 25

Emissions in millions of metric tons per year (1 metric ton = .91 ton)

Worldwide Harmful Emissions of Fossil Fuels

areas, intensive irrigation is washing the nutrients from the soil, leaving it encrusted with salts. This salinized land is unsuitable for raising crops or grazing livestock.

Finally, take a look at the map above, which shows worldwide harmful emissions of fossil fuels (coal, oil, or natural gas). Here you can see how many tons of harmful substances are released into the air by the burning of coal and oil. These harmful emissions contribute to environmental problems such as global warming, the destruction of the ozone layer, and acid rain.

▲ *Above: The United States, Russia, and Asia are responsible for the bulk of the world's fossil fuel emissions.*

◀◀ *Opposite: The coastal pollution along the North, Mediterranean, and Baltic Seas are a result of both factory waste and oil production.*

A Closer Look

You can learn a lot about what a place is like by looking at different kinds of maps, one at a time. However, by comparing the information presented in two or more maps, you can discover something about how and why it got that way.

Compare the climate and land use maps of Europe and the Middle East (pages 17 and 23). How does the climate map help explain the way the land is used in these areas?

Political Map

Arctic Ocean

ICELAND

Atlantic Ocean

NORWAY

SWEDEN

FINLAND

RUSSIA (partial)

ESTONIA

Baltic Sea

LATVIA

North Sea

DENMARK

RUSSIA

LITHUANIA

UNITED KINGDOM

BELARUS

IRELAND

1 GERMANY

POLAND

2

8 UKRAINE

3

7

KAZAKHSTAN (partial)

FRANCE

4

AUSTRIA

HUNGARY

9

6 5

ROMANIA

GEORGIA

Caspian Sea

10

ITALY

13

BULGARIA

Black Sea

12

21 AZERBAIJAN

PORTUGAL

SPAIN

11

GREECE

TURKEY

Mediterranean Sea

14

SYRIA

15

IRAQ

IRAN

16

JORDAN

17

18

19

Persian Gulf

SAUDI ARABIA

20

Red Sea

OMAN

YEMEN

Indian Ocean

Key

1. NETHERLANDS
2. BELGIUM
3. LUXEMBOURG
4. SWITZERLAND
5. CROATIA
6. SLOVENIA
7. SLOVAKIA
8. CZECH REPUBLIC
9. MOLDOVA
10. BOSNIA & HERZEGOVINA
11. ALBANIA
12. MACEDONIA
13. YUGOSLAVIA
14. CYPRUS
15. LEBANON
16. ISRAEL
17. KUWAIT
18. BAHRAIN
19. QATAR
20. UNITED ARAB EMIRATES
21. ARMENIA

Scale

1,000 km

1,000 mi.

Chapter **2**

Mapping People, Cultures, and the Political World

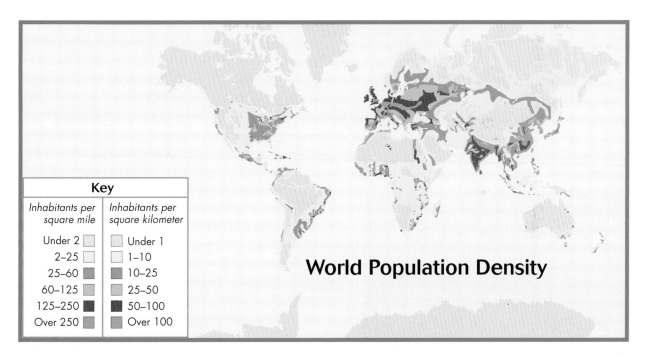

Key	
Inhabitants per square mile	Inhabitants per square kilometer
Under 2	Under 1
2–25	1–10
25–60	10–25
60–125	25–50
125–250	50–100
Over 250	Over 100

World Population Density

Maps can reveal much more about a place than simply what it is like physically. They can also tell you a great deal about the political divisions of the area. Maps can inform you about the cultures and customs of the people who live there as well. They can show the languages spoken in a region, the religions people identify with, and the places where most people live.

▲ *Above: Some of the most populated places in the world are in central and western Europe, India, and southeast China.*

◀◀ *Opposite: The political boundaries of Europe changed dramatically with the fall of Communism in the early 1990s.*

The Political World: Dividing the Land

Political maps such as the one on page 32 are familiar to everyone. In these, there is no attempt to show what an area physically looks like. Rather, a political map shows the boundaries that separate countries (or states and provinces). Colors are used to distinguish one country from another. A political map may also show capitals and major cities, as the map on the opposite page does.

Boundaries are artificial; that is, they are created, set, and changed by people. Conquests, wars, and treaties have all caused boundary changes. Political maps can, therefore, also be a guide to the history of a region.

Geographers keep track of boundary changes, and country and city name changes, as they occur, so that new, up-to-date political maps can be created as soon as possible.

Nature's Influence

The political world is not entirely separate from the natural world. Rivers or mountains may dictate where boundaries are set. Also, if there is a wealth of natural resources in one location, people may try to set boundaries that put all or most of those resources within their own country's borders. Cities, too, are often located according to natural features. Comparing climate and major city maps will show that cities tend to cluster along coastlines or major waterways, and in areas that have less severe climates.

The History and Political Divisions of Europe

From the formation of Greek city-states in the 300s B.C., through two world wars, to the breakup of the Soviet Union in 1991, Europe's map face

▶▶ *Opposite:* Important European and Middle Eastern cities grew up along trade and transportation routes on the coasts and along major waterways.

▼ *Below:* The Golan Heights are a natural land formation that separates Israel and Jordan.

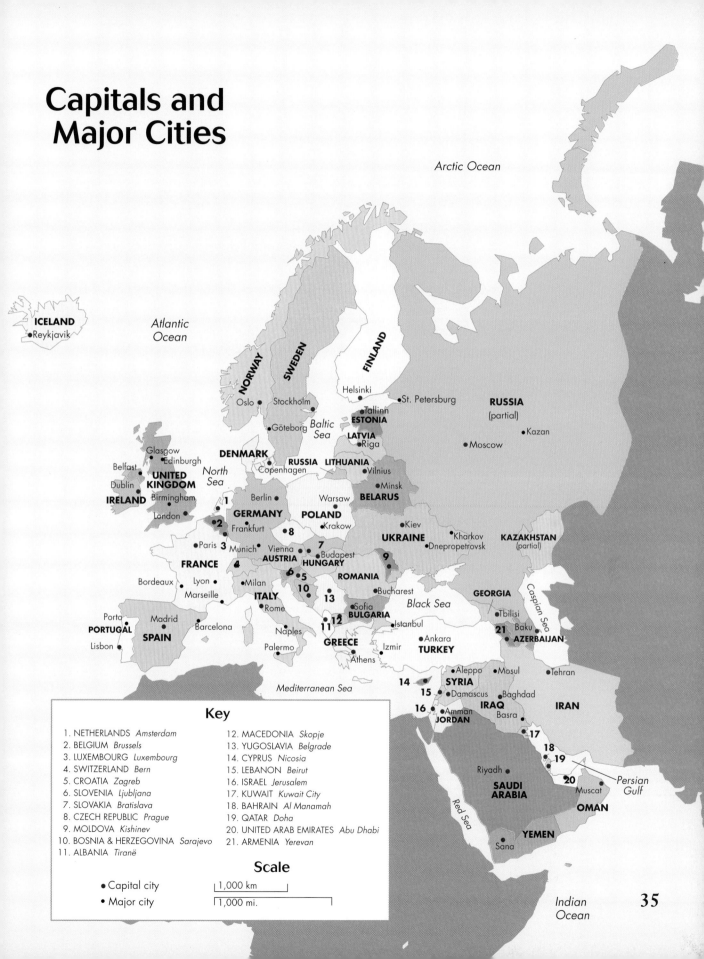

Capitals and Major Cities

Arctic Ocean

ICELAND
•Reykjavik

Atlantic Ocean

NORWAY
Oslo•

SWEDEN
Stockholm•

Göteborg•

Baltic Sea

FINLAND
Helsinki•

•St. Petersburg

Tallinn•
ESTONIA

LATVIA
Riga•

RUSSIA (partial)

•Moscow

•Kazan

Glasgow•
•Edinburgh

Belfast•

DENMARK

Copenhagen•

RUSSIA

LITHUANIA
Vilnius•

North Sea

UNITED KINGDOM

Dublin•
IRELAND
Birmingham•

London•

GERMANY
Berlin•

Frankfurt•

Munich•

Paris• 3

FRANCE

POLAND
Warsaw•
Krakow•

BELARUS
Minsk•

•Kiev

UKRAINE
•Kharkov

•Dnepropetrovsk

KAZAKHSTAN (partial)

1

2

8

7
Vienna•
AUSTRIA
Budapest•
HUNGARY

9

4

5
6

ITALY
Rome•

10

13

ROMANIA
•Bucharest

Bordeaux•
Lyon•

Marseille•

•Milan

GEORGIA
•Tbilisi

Caspian Sea

Porto•

Madrid•

Barcelona•

PORTUGAL

SPAIN

Lisbon•

Naples•

Palermo•

12
11

Sofia•
BULGARIA

GREECE

•Istanbul

Black Sea

Izmir•

•Ankara

TURKEY

21
Baku•
AZERBAIJAN

Athens•

Mediterranean Sea

•Aleppo

•Mosul

•Tehran

14

15

16

SYRIA
•Damascus

•Amman
JORDAN

IRAQ
•Baghdad

Basra•

IRAN

17

18
19

Riyadh•

SAUDI ARABIA

20
Muscat•

OMAN

Persian Gulf

Red Sea

YEMEN

Sana•

Indian Ocean

Key

1. NETHERLANDS *Amsterdam*
2. BELGIUM *Brussels*
3. LUXEMBOURG *Luxembourg*
4. SWITZERLAND *Bern*
5. CROATIA *Zagreb*
6. SLOVENIA *Ljubljana*
7. SLOVAKIA *Bratislava*
8. CZECH REPUBLIC *Prague*
9. MOLDOVA *Kishinev*
10. BOSNIA & HERZEGOVINA *Sarajevo*
11. ALBANIA *Tiranë*

12. MACEDONIA *Skopje*
13. YUGOSLAVIA *Belgrade*
14. CYPRUS *Nicosia*
15. LEBANON *Beirut*
16. ISRAEL *Jerusalem*
17. KUWAIT *Kuwait City*
18. BAHRAIN *Al Manamah*
19. QATAR *Doha*
20. UNITED ARAB EMIRATES *Abu Dhabi*
21. ARMENIA *Yerevan*

Scale

• Capital city
• Major city

⌐ 1,000 km ⌐
⌐ 1,000 mi. ⌐

35

has undergone many changes. Most of these changes reflect a desire for power, or struggles for independence.

The first European political divisions were the city-states of ancient Greece. Athens and Sparta, the most famous of the city-states, were at their heights of power from 500 to 338 B.C.

The study of geography and mapmaking was an important part of ancient Greek life. Although none of the maps from that time have survived, we know about them from ancient Greek writings. Early Greek geographers described and mapped not only their own territories, but as much of the rest of the world as they could piece together through travel, and from their knowledge of astronomy and mathematics. They decided that Earth was round and debated its size. The ancient Greeks were the first people to make maps with lines of latitude and longitude. At about the time that the ancient Greek city-states declined, great empires began to spread across Europe.

The Empires

The first great empire in Europe was the kingdom of Macedonia, north of Greece. Macedonia took control of Greece in 338 B.C. Under the rule of Alexander the Great, Macedonia grew immense, covering the southeastern corner of Europe around the Aegean Sea and extending well into Asia. In Asia, Alexander's empire included, to the east, what is now Turkey, Syria, and northern Iraq and Iran. To the west, his rule extended into Egypt.

By 75 B.C., the Roman Empire was in power. At its height, this empire covered an enormous amount of territory, as you can see from the map on the opposite page. The Romans built roads throughout Europe and made many maps detailing these roads, which were the Romans' lines of communication, travel, and conquest.

In A.D. 395, the Roman Empire split in two. The East Roman Empire, also known as the Byzantine Empire, had Constantinople (now Istanbul, Turkey) as its capital. The West Roman Empire's capital was Rome.

The Roman Empire, Circa A.D. 100

▲ Above: As this map shows, the Roman Empire included all the land surrounding the Mediterranean Sea.

The Middle Ages

With the fall of the West Roman Empire in 476, the Middle Ages began, lasting until the 1500s. During this time, a Germanic tribe called the Franks established a powerful kingdom in the 800s under the rule of Charlemagne the Great. Charlemagne's empire covered an area from what is now northeastern Spain, north to the Baltic Sea and south into the northern half of Italy. About 200 years later, the Holy Roman Empire, ruled by German kings, covered much the same territory, except for France.

As the Roman Catholic Church lost power in Europe, individual kings gained influence and territory for themselves and their kingdoms. By the 1700s, France, Spain, Portugal, The Netherlands, Russia, and Prussia were separate European nations.

The Napoleonic Wars

In 1812, French armies led by Napoleon swept through Europe, conquering most of the mainland. Napoleon's empire took in all of Spain, stretching northeast to the Baltic Sea, east to Russia and the Ottoman Empire in southeast Europe, and south to the foot of Italy. Napoleon lost power when he was defeated at the Battle of Waterloo in 1815.

At this time, European leaders met at the Congress of Vienna to restore their territories and put kings back in power. Many countries' boundaries were changed in the process.

World War I

The next major shift in political power and boundaries came with World War I. The war began in Europe in 1914. France, Italy, Great Britain, and Russia (the Allies) faced off against Germany, Austria-Hungary, and other nations (the Central Powers). The United States joined the Allies in 1917. When the war ended in 1919, Austria-Hungary was divided into several national states, six eastern European nations won independence, and a democratic government replaced Germany's monarchy. In 1922, the Soviet Union was formed.

World War II

World War II began in Europe in 1939. Germany, under the Nazi dictatorship of Adolf Hitler, had taken control of Austria and Czechoslovakia and invaded Poland. Germany, Italy, Japan, and their supporters (the Axis Powers) were opposed in their battle for power by France, Great Britain, the Soviet Union, the United States, and a number of other nations (the Allies). By 1941, Germany and Italy controlled almost all of non-Soviet Europe and that year, Germany began invading the Soviet Union. You can see the large amount of territory occupied by the Germans and their allies by looking at the map of Nazi Europe on the opposite page.

Italy finally fell to the Allied powers in 1943, and Germany in 1945. With the end of the war, the map face of Europe changed once again. Most of the eastern European countries lost their independence, coming under the control of Soviet Communist governments. Germany

Nazi Europe During World War II

Key
- Hitler's Greater Germany
- German allies
- Occupied by Germany/ German allies
- Unoccupied

NORTHERN IRELAND · IRELAND · GREAT BRITAIN · NORWAY · SWEDEN · FINLAND · DENMARK · NETHERLANDS · BELGIUM · LUXEMBOURG · GERMANY · POLAND · SOVIET UNION · CZECHOSLOVAKIA · SLOVAKIA · AUSTRIA · HUNGARY · SWITZERLAND · FRANCE · ROMANIA · YUGOSLAVIA · ITALY · BULGARIA · ALBANIA · GREECE · TURKEY · IRAN · PORTUGAL · SPAIN · SYRIA · LEBANON · IRAQ · PALESTINE · TRANS JORDAN · ALGERIA · TUNISIA · FRENCH MOROCCO · LIBYA · EGYPT

Baltic Sea · North Sea · Atlantic Ocean · Black Sea · Caspian Sea · Mediterranean Sea

▲ Above: During World War II, most of Europe was occupied by Germany and its supporters.

became a divided country—East Germany was Communist, West Germany was non-Communist.

The Fall of Communism

By the late 1980s, reform movements spread throughout the Communist-controlled eastern European countries. These led to elections that put an end to Communist rule in Poland, Hungary, Czechoslovakia, East Germany, Romania, and Bulgaria. East and West Germany united as a non-Communist nation in 1990.

In 1991, Communist rule ended in the Soviet Union, and the Union itself was disbanded. The 12 republics that had made up the Soviet Union became independent countries.

By early 1992, four of the six Yugoslavian republics—Bosnia and Herzegovina (which is one country), Croatia, Macedonia, and Slovenia—had become independent, non-Communist nations.

The remaining republics—Serbia and Montenegro—united to form a new Yugoslavia. In 1993, the two Czechoslovakian republics became separate countries—the Czech Republic and Slovakia. The political boundaries as shown on the map on page 32 were now in place.

Although the boundaries of western Europe seem secure, those of eastern Europe may undergo further changes. Ethnic fighting, such as that in Bosnia and Herzegovina (1992–95), has been a problem, and it is possible that breakaway countries will result.

▲ **Above:** *A man chips away a memento of the Berlin Wall, which once divided the city between two countries.*

The History and Political Divisions of the Middle East

Three civilizations originally occupied most of the Middle East: the Egyptians in the Nile valley, the Babylonians in the area between the Tigris and Euphrates Rivers in what is now Iraq, and the Hittites in what is now Turkey. These were the major ruling empires during the period from about 3500 B.C. to the 800s B.C.

One Empire

As we saw earlier in this chapter, Alexander the Great extended his empire from Greece and southeastern Europe into the Middle East in 331 B.C. What are now Turkey, Syria, and northern Iraq, plus Egypt, came under the control of a single empire. The Romans gained control of the area by 30 B.C. The map on page 37 shows the boundaries of the Roman Empire at the height of its power.

Islamic Rule

In the A.D. 600s, Arab Muslims from what is now Saudi Arabia conquered the region that includes present-day Egypt, Iran, Iraq, and Syria. The next great ruling power to gain control in the area was the Ottoman Empire. This empire arose in the 1300s in what is now Turkey. By the early 1500s, the Ottoman Turks had conquered the Arab-held lands of the Middle East.

Because Islamic traders traveled by water a great deal, mapmakers during this period concentrated on mapping newer, more accurate sea charts. Arab travelers to Africa and Asia brought back information that was added to land maps of these regions.

World War I

During World War I, the Turks fought on the side of Germany and the other Central Powers. The Arabs, who objected to Turkish rule, supported the Allies. They did this because Britain promised to create independent Arab states once the war was won.

In 1923, the Ottoman Empire was defeated, and the Republic of Turkey was formed. However, the Arab lands didn't become independent states. Instead, the League of Nations divided the area into mandated territories under European rule. Lebanon and Syria came under French rule, and Iraq, Jordan, and Palestine came under British rule. At this point, most of the boundaries of today's Middle East were in place. By 1946, Lebanon, Syria, Iraq, and Jordan had gained their independence.

Palestine Divided

In 1947, the division of Palestine created new boundaries and also problems that continue to trouble the region. Jews had moved into Palestine in the 1920s and 1930s with the intention of establishing a homeland there. This angered the Arabs, who wanted Palestine to be only an Arab state. And neither the Jews nor the Arabs wanted the British in control. In 1947, after a series of wars, the United Nations divided the country into an Arab state (Palestine) and a Jewish state. The Jews named their state Israel.

Again war broke out between the Arabs and the Jews. By the time the war ended in 1949, Israel had taken control of most of the area, and Egypt and Jordan occupied the rest. Palestine no longer existed on the map, although the Arabs continued to call their occupied lands by that name. Arab-Israeli conflicts have continued, along with boundary changes, to the present time.

Population, Language, and Religion

Most countries' governments conduct a census (population count) on some sort of regular basis. The United States, for example, has conducted a regular ten-year census since 1790.

Census figures are used to make maps that show how population is distributed. The world population density map on page 33 is one such map. By compiling statistics over a period of years—from census and birth and death records—geographers can make predictions regarding population growth, as shown in the world map below.

Because many different languages may be spoken in any one country, it is difficult to map language distribution precisely. However, large areas that represent language families can be mapped, as shown on the map on the opposite page. In the same way, predominant religions of an area can also be mapped, as shown in the world religions map on the same page.

▶▶ *Opposite: The Middle East's dominant language group (Afro-Asiatic) and religion (Sunni Muslim) are the same as those of North Africa.*

▼ *Below: Europe, northern Asia, and the United States have relatively stable populations with little growth.*

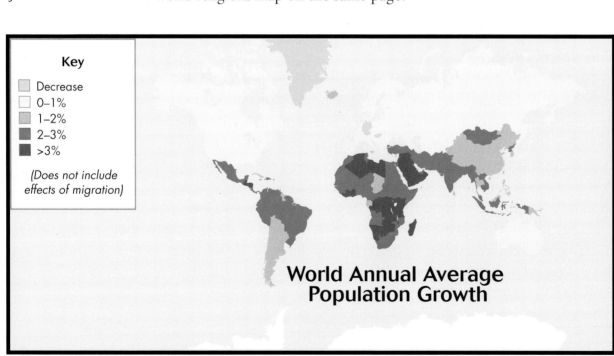

Key
- Decrease
- 0–1%
- 1–2%
- 2–3%
- >3%

(Does not include effects of migration)

World Annual Average Population Growth

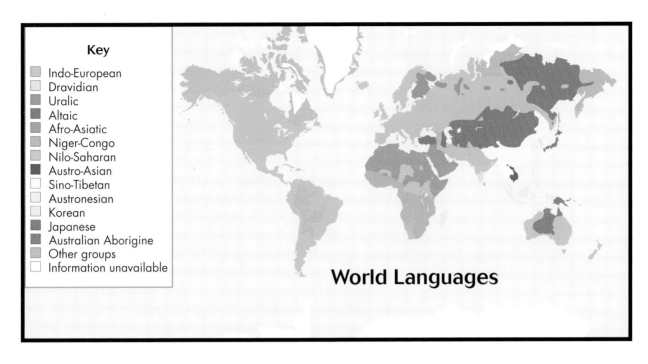

Key

- Indo-European
- Dravidian
- Uralic
- Altaic
- Afro-Asiatic
- Niger-Congo
- Nilo-Saharan
- Austro-Asian
- Sino-Tibetan
- Austronesian
- Korean
- Japanese
- Australian Aborigine
- Other groups
- Information unavailable

World Languages

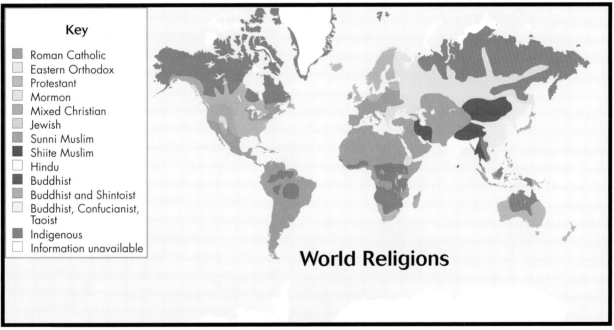

Key

- Roman Catholic
- Eastern Orthodox
- Protestant
- Mormon
- Mixed Christian
- Jewish
- Sunni Muslim
- Shiite Muslim
- Hindu
- Buddhist
- Buddhist and Shintoist
- Buddhist, Confucianist, Taoist
- Indigenous
- Information unavailable

World Religions

The Religions of Europe and the Middle East

Although there is a great deal of ethnic variety in Europe and the
Middle East, only a handful of religions are important there. A look
at the map on page 44 will show how they are distributed.

Religions

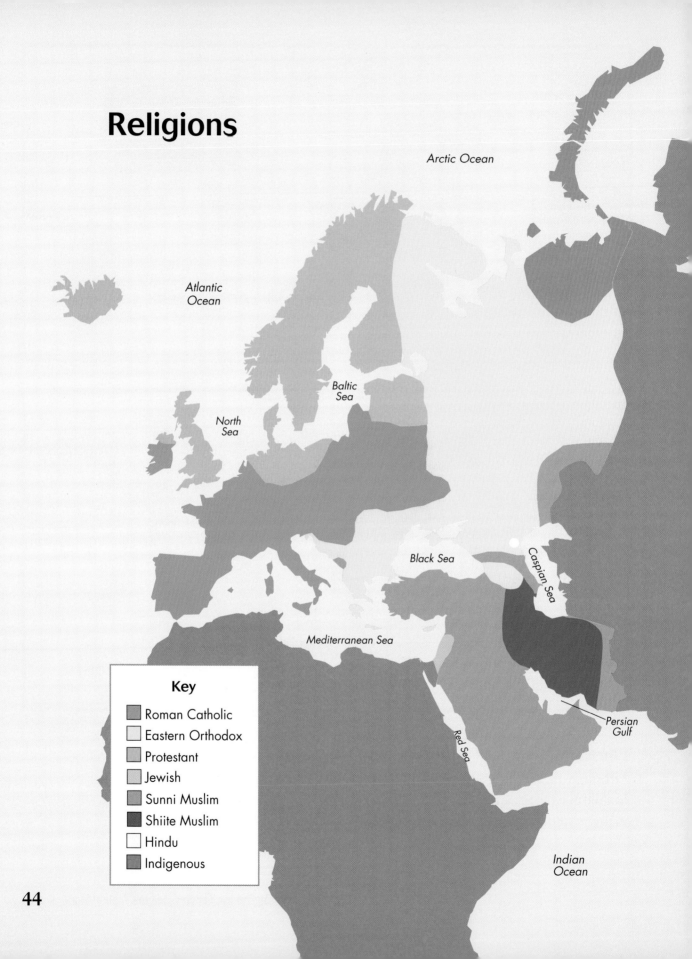

Arctic Ocean

Atlantic
Ocean

Baltic
Sea

North
Sea

Black Sea

Caspian Sea

Mediterranean Sea

Red Sea

Persian
Gulf

Indian
Ocean

Key

- Roman Catholic
- Eastern Orthodox
- Protestant
- Jewish
- Sunni Muslim
- Shiite Muslim
- Hindu
- Indigenous

Left: *Young Hasidic Jews sit with an elder at the Wailing Wall—the remains of an ancient and revered temple.*

Opposite: *Israel is the only country in the world that is predominantly Jewish. It is surrounded by Muslim countries.*

In Europe, most people observe Christian religions. The southern part of western Europe and most of central Europe are Roman Catholic. This reflects the enormous importance of the Roman Catholic Church in this area during the Middle Ages.

The northern countries of western Europe are primarily Protestant, with the exception of Ireland. Two-thirds of the people in Northern Ireland, which is part of the United Kingdom of Great Britain, are Protestant, while most citizens of Ireland, an independent country, are Catholic. This religious division has been the cause of violent conflicts in Northern Ireland since the mid-1960s.

The majority of Russians and those living in southeastern Europe are Eastern Orthodox.

Three of the world's major religions—Christianity, Judaism, and Islam—began in the Middle East, and they are still represented there today. Georgia, Armenia, and Cyprus are predominantly Eastern Orthodox; Israel is Jewish. The rest of the Middle Eastern countries are Muslim. Most of the Muslim population is Sunni Muslim, except in Iran, where Shiite Muslims are in the majority.

The Languages of Europe and the Middle East

Despite the many different languages that are spoken throughout Europe and the Middle East, most are a part of one language family: Indo-European. If you look at the map on page 46, you will see that this language family, colored light green, covers nearly all of Europe,

Languages

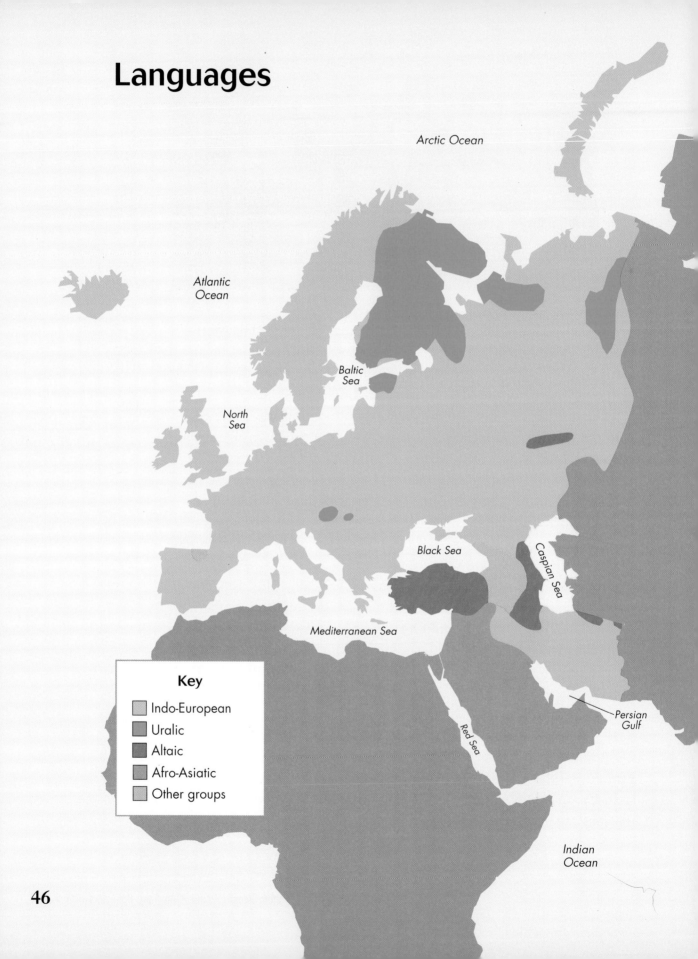

Arctic Ocean

Atlantic
Ocean

Baltic
Sea

North
Sea

Black Sea

Caspian
Sea

Mediterranean Sea

Persian
Gulf

Red Sea

Indian
Ocean

Key

Indo-European

Uralic

Altaic

Afro-Asiatic

Other groups

plus Iran in the Middle East. In Europe, three major language groups of the Indo-European language family are spoken.

Germanic languages, such as English, German, Danish, and Swedish, are spoken mainly in the northern countries. Romance languages, which include Italian, Spanish, and French, are spoken in the south. Balto-Slavic languages, such as Russian, Czech, Polish, and Bulgarian, are spoken throughout eastern Europe. In Iran, the people speak Farsi, which is a Persian language. Persian is an Indo-Iranian language—another branch of the Indo-European language family.

The other major language family found in Europe is Uralic, represented by the Finnish language. Other language families in the Middle East include Altaic (blue on the map) and Afro-Asiatic (dark pink). The Turkish languages spoken in Turkey and Azerbaijan are Altaic. Arabic—the major language in the rest of the Middle East— is an Afro-Asiatic language.

Population and Income in Europe and the Middle East

Population

In 1996, the estimated population of Europe was more than 700 million people. Russia has the highest population of any European country, almost 120 million. But because Russia covers such a large area and has few major cities, the country's overall population density is not very high compared with the nations of western Europe (see the map on page 48). As a continent, Europe ranks second to Asia as the most densely populated continent in the world. By looking at the population growth map on page 49, however, you can see that Europe's population is very stable—and even shrinking in some areas.

Although the Middle East is not densely populated, it has a high growth rate. In the early 1980s, the population was about 164 million. It is estimated that by the year 2000, the population will be 254 million. This is a 55 percent increase in less than 20 years.

◀◀ *Opposite: The Finnish are among the few European peoples who speak a Uralic, rather than an Indo-European, language.*

Income

Gross domestic product (GDP) is the total output of a country—all its products and labor. Dividing the value of a country's GDP by its population gives the per capita (per person) GDP. This figure represents the average annual income of that country's people. Generally speaking, the most industrialized countries have the highest GDP.

In Europe, for example, Albania had an estimated per capita GDP of $1,110 in 1994. Germany, which is much more industrialized, had a 1995 per capita GDP of $28,250.

▶ **Right:** *If you compare this map with the climate map on page 17, you'll notice that the regions with the gentlest climate have the densest population.*

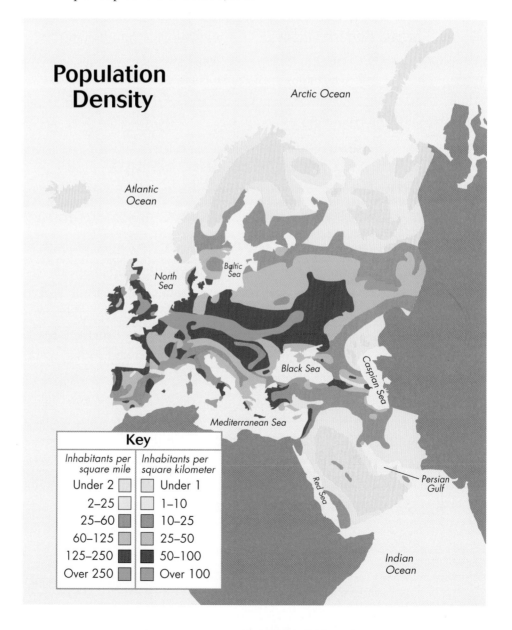

Population
Density

Arctic Ocean

Atlantic
Ocean

North
Sea

Baltic
Sea

Black Sea

Caspian Sea

Mediterranean Sea

Red Sea

Persian
Gulf

Indian
Ocean

Key	
Inhabitants per square mile	Inhabitants per square kilometer
Under 2	Under 1
2–25	1–10
25–60	10–25
60–125	25–50
125–250	50–100
Over 250	Over 100

Average Annual Population Growth

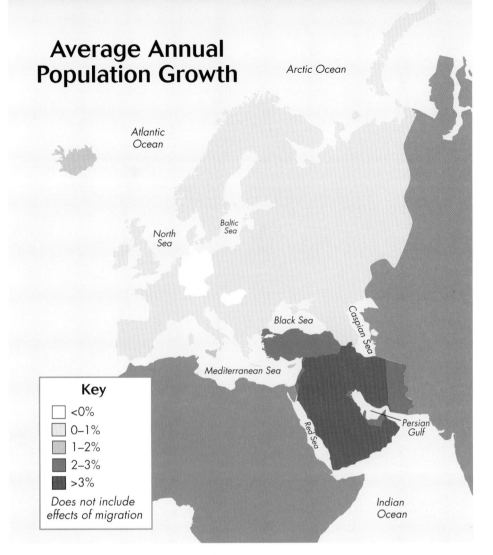

Arctic Ocean

Atlantic Ocean

North Sea

Baltic Sea

Black Sea

Caspian Sea

Mediterranean Sea

Red Sea

Persian Gulf

Indian Ocean

Key

- ☐ <0%
- ☐ 0–1%
- ☐ 1–2%
- ☐ 2–3%
- ■ >3%

Does not include effects of migration

◄ **Left:** *Although the Arabian Peninsula is not densely populated, its population is growing very quickly, as you can see on this map.*

Of the major oil-producing countries in the Middle East, the United Arab Emirates had an estimated 1994 per capita GDP of $22,470. Turkey, which is not dependent on oil and has a more diverse economy, had an estimated 1994 per capita GDP of $4,910.

A Closer Look

Look at the map of the Roman Empire on page 37. It covered an enormous amount of territory. But just how much land did the Romans occupy in today's terms? Compare this map to the political map of Europe and the Middle East that appears on page 32. List the countries of today that would have been included in the Roman Empire of A.D. 109. How does the size of the empire compare to the territory occupied by the Nazis in World War II (see the map on page 39)?

49

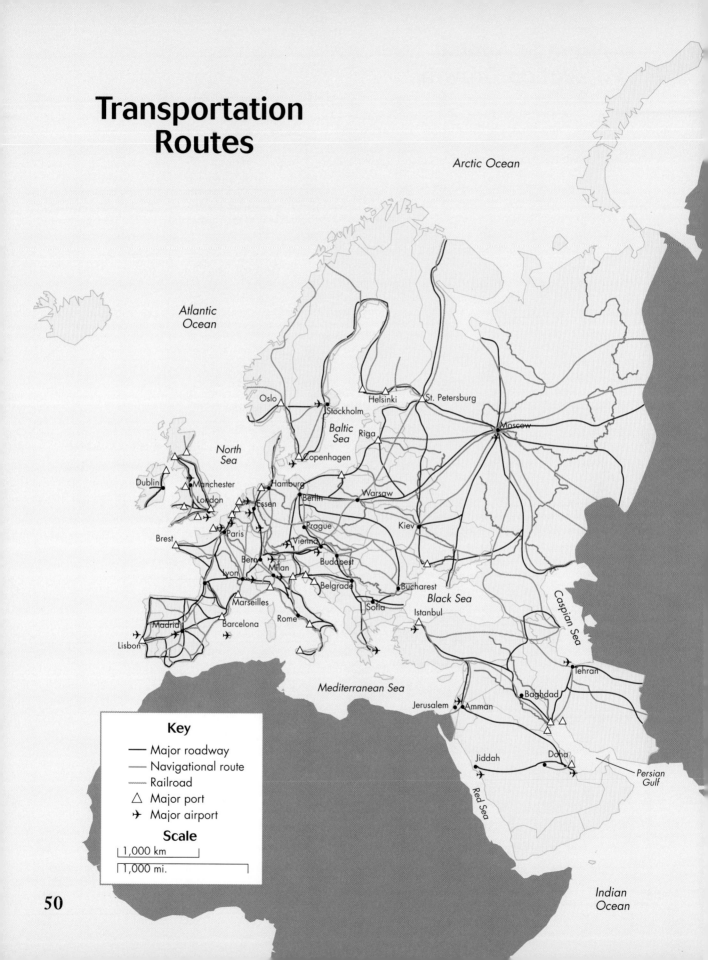

Transportation
Routes

Arctic Ocean

*Atlantic
Ocean*

Oslo
Stockholm
*Baltic
Sea*
Helsinki
St. Petersburg
Moscow
Riga
Copenhagen
*North
Sea*
Hamburg
Warsaw
Dublin
Manchester
Essen
Berlin
London
Prague
Kiev
Brest
Paris
Vienna
Bern
Milan
Budapest
Lyon
Belgrade
Bucharest
Black Sea
Marseilles
Sofia
Madrid
Barcelona
Rome
Istanbul
*Caspian
Sea*
Lisbon
Tehran
Mediterranean Sea
Baghdad
Jerusalem
Amman
*Persian
Gulf*
Jiddah
Doha
*Red
Sea*
*Indian
Ocean*

Key

— Major roadway
— Navigational route
--- Railroad
△ Major port
✈ Major airport

Scale
|‒ 1,000 km ‒|
|‒ 1,000 mi. ‒|

3

Mapping the World Through Which We Move

In addition to showing us the physical and political characteristics of the world, maps can also have a more practical, "hands on" purpose: They can assist us in moving through our world. Whether that world is an entire continent, a single city, or the second floor of an art museum, different maps provide us with the information we need to get from one point to another.

Maps Show the Way

Whenever we want to get from one place to another, maps can help us plan our routes by showing the options that are available. Maps show where roads are located and what kind of roads they are. They can also tell us whether we can take an airplane, train, bus, or other form of transportation to get there. Once we reach our destination, maps again can help us plan how best to get around—on foot, by car, or by some kind of public transportation.

Creating Road and City Maps

To create road maps and city maps, mapmakers (cartographers) look first for base data maps that accurately position points to be included on the new map. These base maps might be acquired from the

◀◀*Opposite: Western Europe has many roadways and other transportation routes to service its cities.*

Federal government, states, or cities. Aerial photographs may be taken to show if, and how, any areas may have changed since the base map was made.

Then, cartographers contact agencies that can provide specific information about street names—the names that are used locally—that will be the most help to a person traveling in the area. Other agencies are contacted to determine which buildings or other points of interest are important and should be included on the map of the area. Field work—actually visiting the area being mapped—adds useful first-hand information.

The Importance of Scale

Choosing the right scale for a map is an important step in making sure that the map will be as useful as possible.

To help people find their way around downtown Boston, for example, a cartographer would design a large-scale map that gives a close-up view of all the streets. But suppose someone wanted to drive from Philadelphia in eastern Pennsylvania to Pittsburgh in western Pennsylvania. Then a small-scale road map of the entire state would be more helpful than large-scale maps of all the cities between Philadelphia and Pittsburgh.

Scale also plays an important part in determining what is shown on a map. The smaller the scale, the more carefully cartographers must pick and choose the details that are being included. Careful selection is needed in order to keep a map from becoming too cluttered.

The transportation and city maps in this chapter provide still more ways to look at and learn about the continent, countries, and cities.

Transportation in Europe and the Middle East

A look at the map on page 50 shows a maze of major transportation routes throughout most of Europe, but far fewer routes in the Middle East. Some of this difference can be explained by topography, some of it by demand.

Roads

Western Europe has one of the best, and densest, road systems in the world, matching the density of its population. One reason for Europe's thick network of roads is that there are a great many important cities in a very small area, most of which have been linked for centuries for military and trade purposes. Today, many people travel between these cities in cars, including vacationers from around the world. Trucks transport goods throughout western Europe, and many of the major cities are linked not only with each other, but also with various ocean or sea ports.

Moving east, the road systems become less dense as cities become less crowded together. In eastern Europe, there are fewer residents and tourists using the roads. Instead, major roadways are used mostly by trucks carrying freight. Since the breakup of the Soviet Union, however, car ownership is becoming more common in the former Communist countries, and tourism is also on the rise. The road system in eastern Europe is sure to change in the coming years to handle these increases.

In the Middle East, large expanses of desert and fewer cities than in Europe mean fewer major roadways as well. Buses are an important form of transportation both inside and outside the cities, and trucks are used to transport goods.

Railroads

Railroads were built first in Europe. In 1804, the first steam loco-motive was used in Wales to haul coal at a mine. In 1825, the first regularly scheduled public freight service on rails opened in England. In 1830, the first regular public passenger service began. Today Europe has about a fourth of the world's railroad tracks, and trains are still used to carry both freight and people. Passenger trains are a common and very popular form of transportation throughout Europe, particularly in western Europe, where cities are relatively close together.

▲ *Above:* Venice's canals add to the beauty of this old city.

As you can see from the transportation map on page 50, the Middle East does not have an extensive railroad system. But major freight lines link important ports on the Black, Caspian, and Mediterranean Seas, and the Persian Gulf.

Waterways

The many rivers and canals that crisscross Europe have been used as transportation routes for hundreds of years. They are still important today, as the transportation map shows. Barges and ships use these waterways to carry freight between the major inland cities of Europe and its ports. The city of Venice, in Italy, is unusual because it is totally dependent on its waterways. Venice's "roads" are all canals.

Europe's irregular coastline offers many natural harbors. This has helped Europe become important in the shipping trade. Rotterdam, in The Netherlands, is one of the world's busiest ports. Among other leading port cities are Hamburg, Germany; London, England; and Marseilles, France.

Only two major river systems serve the Middle East: the Tigris-Euphrates in Syria and Iraq, and the Nile in Egypt. These rivers provide important transportation routes for cargo, connecting with major seaports in the Persian Gulf and Mediterranean Sea.

Airlines

All the major cities of Europe are connected by airlines, and European airlines fly all over the world. KLM, the Royal Dutch Airlines of The Netherlands, is the world's oldest commercial airline in service. Airlines also operate out of the largest cities of the Middle East, and provide an essential means of transportation over the long stretches of desert and impassable mountains.

Other Transportation

Cars, buses, and taxis provide transportation in the cities of both Europe and the Middle East. Many European cities also have extensive subway (underground rail) systems. A great many Europeans own motorcycles or motor bikes, which can thread through the narrow streets of Europe's old cities more easily than cars. Bicycles are also a popular form of transportation. In the Middle East, huge pipelines provide a special transportation system for the oil produced there.

The Cities of Europe and the Middle East

Many European and Middle Eastern cities have "old town" sections that are many hundreds of years old. These major cities often share two other traits as well: They were built on rivers, and they were walled. Walls provided protection by cutting the cities off from easy access to enemies. Rivers made an approaching enemy who was traveling by boat easy to spot. In addition, the rivers provided transportation and trade routes.

Vatican City

Entirely surrounded by Rome, the capital of Italy, is Vatican City. It is the center of the Roman Catholic Church (see the map below).

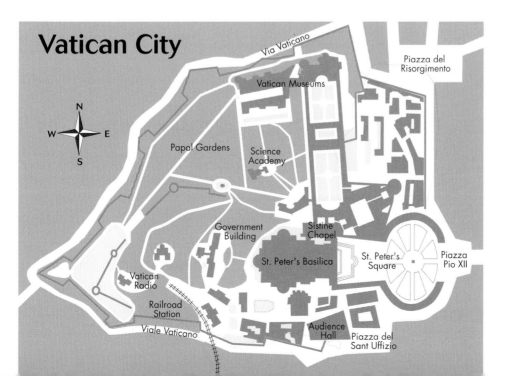

◄ *Left:* Vatican City is Europe's only remaining city-state.

This walled-city-within-a-city is an independent state, which makes it the smallest country in the world. The Vatican's ruler is the Pope. The Vatican has its own currency, radio station, army, and postal and telephone systems. St. Peter's Basilica, which is easy to spot on the map of Vatican City on page 55, is one of the world's most famous churches. It was built in the early 1500s. The Sistine Chapel, with its ceiling painted by Michelangelo, and the Vatican Museums, north of the chapel, are visited by thousands of tourists every year.

Vienna

Vienna, the capital of Austria, is located on a river—a branch of the Danube called the Danube Canal. The city was founded and encircled by walls in about A.D. 100. As it grew, new sets of walls were put up around it. In 1857, the third set of walls was torn down and replaced by the Ringstrasse, or Ring Street. The street is subdivided into individually named sections, such as Opernring and Burg Ring, as you can see on the map on the opposite page. By following Ring Street, you will see where the last of Vienna's boundary walls were located.

St. Stephen's Cathedral marks the center of Vienna, and from its 450-foot tower you can view the whole city. To the east is one of the houses in which the eighteenth-century composer Wolfgang Amadeus Mozart lived. While there, he wrote *The Marriage of Figaro*, which is why the house is called Figaro-haus in German. Tourists visit Hoher Markt square to see the mechanical figures on the huge Anker Clock go into motion each noon. Among the many

▼ *Below: In downtown Vienna, a modern building with a glass facade reflects much older, neighboring buidlings.*

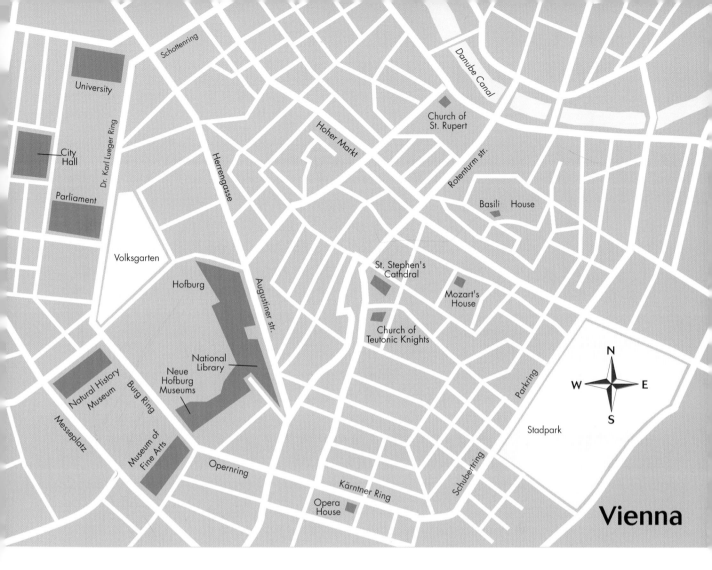

Vienna

landmark buildings located on the Ringstrasse is the Hofburg—the Imperial Palace. This enormous building includes the royal apartments of the Hapsburgs (Austria's last royal family), treasuries, the National Library, several museums, and the Spanish Riding School, where the world-famous dancing Lipizzan stallions are trained.

▲ **Above:** *The Burg Ring, Opernring, and other segments of the Ringstrasse encircle the old section of Vienna.*

Jerusalem

Jerusalem, the capital of Israel, is a holy city for Jews, Christians, and Muslims. The holiest places, and major landmarks, are found inside the high stone walls of Old Jerusalem (see the map on page 59). The walls were built in the 1500s, but parts of the Old City date back to the first century B.C. Today, seven gates give access to Old Jerusalem.

The Golden Gate, in the east wall, is blocked off. The Jaffa Gate, in the west wall, is the one most tourists use. Here you find the Citadel, a fortified area of the wall and the location of the state-of-the-art Tower of David Museum. This museum tells visitors the history of Jerusalem.

Four of the most important landmarks in Old Jerusalem are the Wailing Wall, El-Aqsa Mosque, the Dome of the Rock, in the eastern part of the city, and the Church of the Holy Sepulchre, to the west. The Wailing (or Western) Wall is an important Jewish shrine, and El Aqsa Mosque is holy to the Muslims. The Dome of the Rock is a beautiful seventh-century mosque with a golden dome. The building covers a rock that has religious significance for both Muslims and Jews. The Church of the Holy Sepulchre is important to Christians because it is believed to stand on the place where Christ was put to death.

▼ *Below:* The famous Dome of the Rock is one of the most beautiful landmarks in Israel.

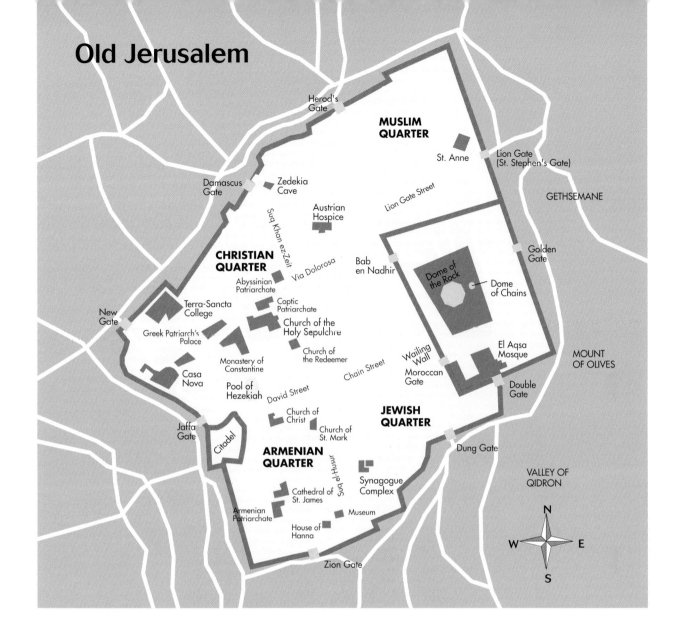

Old Jerusalem

Herod's Gate

MUSLIM QUARTER

St. Anne

Lion Gate (St. Stephen's Gate)

GETHSEMANE

Damascus Gate

Zedekia Cave

Lion Gate Street

Austrian Hospice

Suq Khan ezZeit

CHRISTIAN QUARTER

Via Dolorosa

Bab en Nadhir

Golden Gate

Dome of the Rock

Dome of Chains

Abyssinian Patriarchate

Terra-Sancta College

Coptic Patriarchate

Church of the Holy Sepulchre

Greek Patriarch's Palace

New Gate

Church of the Redeemer

Monastery of Constantine

El Aqsa Mosque

MOUNT OF OLIVES

Casa Nova

Pool of Hezekiah

David Street

Wailing Wall

Chain Street

Moroccan Gate

Double Gate

Jaffa Gate

Citadel

Church of Christ

Church of St. Mark

JEWISH QUARTER

Dung Gate

VALLEY OF QIDRON

ARMENIAN QUARTER

Suq el-Husur

Synagogue Complex

Cathedral of St. James

Museum

Armenian Patriarchate

House of Hanna

Zion Gate

N
W · E
S

Other Maps and Guides

In addition to road and city street maps, there are many other maps and guides that are useful to us in moving through the world. There are navigational charts for boaters, and transportation maps such as air, rail, and bus route maps. There are maps that show special points of interest, such as all the caves in a state or all the parks or monuments in a city. Floor plans that guide you through famous buildings and museums are another kind of map. And there are trail guides for hikers, bikers, skiers, and horseback riders.

▲ *Above: Jerusalem is filled with holy places of great religious significance for Christians, Jews, and Muslims.*

However you choose to get around our vast and complicated world—and wherever you choose to go—you will always find that maps will help you do it much more easily.

Getting Around Aboveground and Underground

The scale of the maps you have been looking at give you a rough idea of how a city is laid out and the location of some of its landmarks. This type of map can help you start to plan your visit to a city. A larger-scale map, like the one of the Louvre Museum in Paris, shown below, allows you to zero in on a particular area and see more clearly how to get around. For example, by looking at this map, you can see the general plan of the Louvre. On a city map such as the others in this chapter, the museum would be simply a block of color.

The map of the London subway on the opposite page gives still another view of a European city. This map shows how to get around London using the underground train system (known in London as the

▶ *Right:* *The Louvre surrounds courtyards, a garden, and a pyramid-shaped entrance leading underground.*

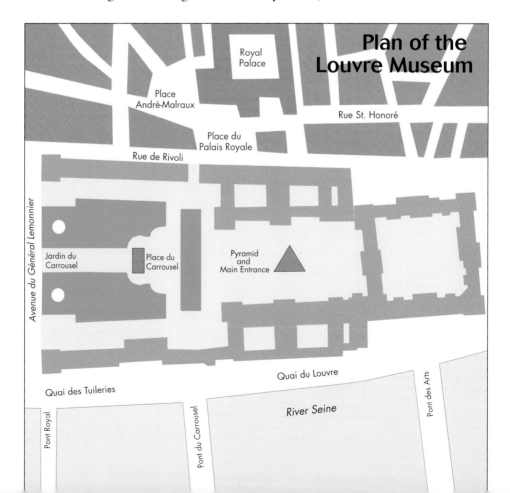

Plan of the Louvre Museum

Royal Palace

Place André-Malraux

Rue St. Honoré

Place du Palais Royale

Rue de Rivoli

Avenue du Général Lemonnier

Jardin du Carrousel

Place du Carrousel

Pyramid and Main Entrance

Quai du Louvre

Quai des Tuileries

Pont des Arts

Pont Royal

Pont du Carrousel

River Seine

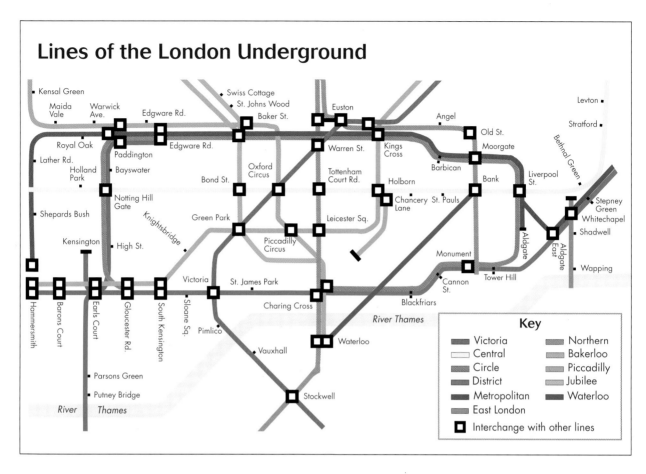

Lines of the London Underground

Tube). This kind of map—usually used for city subway or bus routes—is known as a linear map. A linear map doesn't try to show things as they are; it makes them simpler. In real life, these routes do not all travel in straight lines, and stops are not evenly spaced. But a map such as this, using straight lines and different colors for the different routes, helps you to easily see the stops along each train line.

▲ *Above:* Here is a partial map of the London Underground system, which is drawn as a linear map.

A Closer Look

Many maps—such as road or city maps—are especially designed to give us a closer look at a place. They tell us how to get around or what we can expect to see.

Look at the map of Vatican City on page 55. You can see from this map not only the buildings and grounds around the Vatican, but also the way the rooms are laid out within the Vatican itself. Using this type of viewpoint and scale, make a map of your school or school grounds.

Glossary

acid rain Rain that has collected waste gases from the atmosphere and is damaging to the environment.

cash crop A crop that is grown to be sold.

city-state A political unit made up of a city and its surrounding territory.

colonization Occupying another country to use its resources.

Communism A way of organizing a country so that all property and businesses are owned by the government or community and profits are shared by everyone.

deciduous trees Trees that shed their leaves every year.

deforestation Large-scale clearing of forested land, which may die as a result.

desertification The creation of desert conditions as a result of long droughts, overgrazing, or soil erosion.

drought A long period without rainfall.

erosion Wearing away by the action of wind or water.

export Something sold to another country.

global warming A gradual rise in the temperature of Earth's atmosphere.

gross domestic product (GDP) The total output of a country; all products and labor.

hardwood Broadleaf trees (see **softwood**).

indigenous Original to a particular place.

industrialized countries Countries with a lot of industry.

latitude A horizontal line used on maps to mark the distance of a place from the equator.

lichen A flat, often greenish growth on trees and rocks.

longitude A vertical line used on maps to mark the distance of a place from the Greenwich Observatory in England.

oasis (plural, oases) A fertile area in a desert.

per capita Per person (literally, "per head").

plateau A large, mostly level, area of land that is higher than the land surrounding it.

salinization The process by which nutrients are washed from the soil by over-irrigation, leaving the soil encrusted with salts.

softwood Coniferous, or cone-bearing, trees.

tundra A cold area with no trees. Beneath the surface of the ground is a layer of permanently frozen soil.

Further Reading

Circling the Globe, Vols. 1, 2, & 7. Austin, TX: Raintree Steck-Vaughn, 1995.

Encyclopedia of World Geography, Vols. 6–15. New York: Marshall Cavendish, 1994.

Harvey, Miles. *The Fall of the Soviet Union*. Danbury, CT: Children's Press, 1995.

King, John. *Conflict in the Middle East*. New York: New Discovery Books, 1993.

Land and Peoples, Vols. 2–4. Danbury, CT: Grolier, Inc., 1997.

McLeish, Ewan. *Europe*. Austin, TX: Raintree Steck-Vaughn, 1997.

Index

Page numbers for illustrations are in boldface.

Animals,
    of Europe, 18–19, **19**
    of Middle East, 20
Arabian Peninsula, 15, 16

Boundaries
    of Europe, 11–12

of Middle East, 12

Climate, **11**, 15, 16–18, **17**, 20–21, 34

Energy
    consumption, 26, **28**, **29**

production, 26, **27**, **29**
environmental damage, 19, 26,
    28–31, **30**, **31**

History, European
    Communism, 38–39
    empires, 36–38, **37**
    Middle Ages, 37
    wars, 37–39
    See also Political boundaries,
        influence of history on
History, Middle Eastern
    empires, 40–41
    Islamic rule, 40–41
    Palestine, 41–42
    World War I, 41

Jerusalem, 57–59, **59**

Land use, 21–24, **23**, **24**
    crops, 22, 24
languages, 42, **43**, 45–47, **46**
London Tube (subway), 60–61,
    61
Louvre, **60**

Mapping
    art of, 7–8
    early study of, 36
    Earth, **8–9**, 36
    roads and cities, 51–52, **55**,
        57, **59**
    terms, 6–7
    See also Maps
maps
    importance of, 6
    kinds of, 5–6, **6**, 59, 61

reading of, 9
scale in, 7, 9, 52, 60
    See also Political maps;
        mapping
mineral resources, 22, 24–26, **25**

Nazi Europe, 38–39, **39**

Physical map. *See* Topography
plants
    of Europe, **19**
    of Middle East, 20
political boundaries, 33
    influence of history on, 34,
        36–42, **40**
    influence of nature on, **34**
political maps, **32**, 33
    capitals and major cities, 34,
        35
    definition of, 34
    See also Political boundaries
population growth and density,
    20–21, **33**, **42**, 47, **48**, **49**

Religions, 42, **43–45**

Topography, **10**, 12–15, 20–21, 52
transportation, 21, **50**, 51, 52
    airlines, 54
    alternative, 55
    railroads, 53–54
    roads, 53
    subway and bus, **61**
    waterways, **54**

Vatican City, 55–56, **55**
Vienna, **56–57**